World Book's Learning Ladders
Wild Animals

WORLD
BOOK

a Scott Fetzer company
Chicago
www.worldbookonline.com

World Book, Inc.
180 North LaSalle Street
Suite 900
Chicago, Illinois 60601
USA

For information about other World Book publications, visit our website at www.worldbook.com or call **1-800-WORLDBK (967-5325)**.

For information about sales to schools and libraries, call **1-800-975-3250 (United States)**; **1-800-837-5365 (Canada)**.

2008 revised printing

Library of Congress Cataloging-in-Publication Data

Wild animals.
    p. cm. -- (World Book's learning ladders)
  Summary: "Introduction to wild animals that live in Africa using simple text, question and answer format, illustrations, and photos. Features include puzzles and games, fun facts, a resource list, and an index"--Provided by publisher.
  Includes bibliographical references and index.
  ISBN 978-0-7166-7733-8
  1. Animals--Africa--Juvenile literature.
I. World Book, Inc.
QL336.W47 2007
591.96--dc22
                    2007018920

World Book's Learning Ladders
ISBN 978-0-7166-7725-3 (set, hc.)

Also available as:
ISBN 978-0-7166-7776-5 (e-book, Learning Hub)
ISBN 978-0-7166-7777-2 (e-book, Spindle)
ISBN 978-0-7166-7778-9 (e-book, EPUB3)
ISBN 978-0-7166-7779-6 (e-book, PDF)

Printed in China by Shenzhen Wing King Tong Paper Products Co, Ltd., Shenzhen, Guangdong
10th printing February 2017

Staff

Executive Committee
President: Jim O'Rourke
Vice President and Editor in Chief: Paul A. Kobasa
Vice President, Finance: Donald D. Keller
Vice President, Marketing: Jean Lin
Vice President, International Sales: Maksim Rutenberg
Director, Human Resources: Bev Ecker

Editorial
Director, Digital & Print Content Development: Emily Kline
Editor, Digital & Print Content Development: Kendra Muntz
Senior Editor: Shawn Brennan
Senior Editor: Dawn Krajcik
Manager, Indexing Services: David Pofelski
Manager, Contracts & Compliance (Rights & Permissions):
    Loranne K. Shields

Digital
Director, Digital Product Development: Erika Meller

Graphics and Design
Senior Art Director: Tom Evans
Coordinator, Design Development and Production: Brenda B. Tropinski

Manufacturing/Pre-Press
Production/Technology Manager: Anne Fritzinger
Proofreader: Nathalie Strassheim

This edition is an adaptation of the Ladders series published originally by T&N Children's Publishing, Inc., of Minnetonka, Minnesota.

Photographic credits: Cover: © Robert Hardholt, Shutterstock; p4: Zefa; p6: Ardea Ltd; p7: Tony Stone Images; p8: Ardea Ltd; p10: Ardea Ltd; p11: Tony Stone Images; p12: Tony Stone Images; p13: Planet Earth Pictures; p16: Oxford Scientific Films; p19: Planet Earth Pictures; p20: BBC Natural History Unit; p22: BBC Natural History Unit; p23: Natural History Photographic Agency.

Illustrators: Peter Utton, Jon Stuart

What's inside?

In this book, you can find out about lots of exciting wild animals. All of the animals in this book live in Africa. They make their homes on dry, grassy land that stretches as far as your eyes can see.

Rhinoceros

A rhinoceros, or rhino for short, lives by itself. It spends the day dozing on the grass, nibbling at plants, and rolling around in wet mud to cool down. All the other animals keep out of its way because it looks so fierce!

A rhino pulls twigs from a bush with its long top lip. It chews the twigs with its flat back teeth.

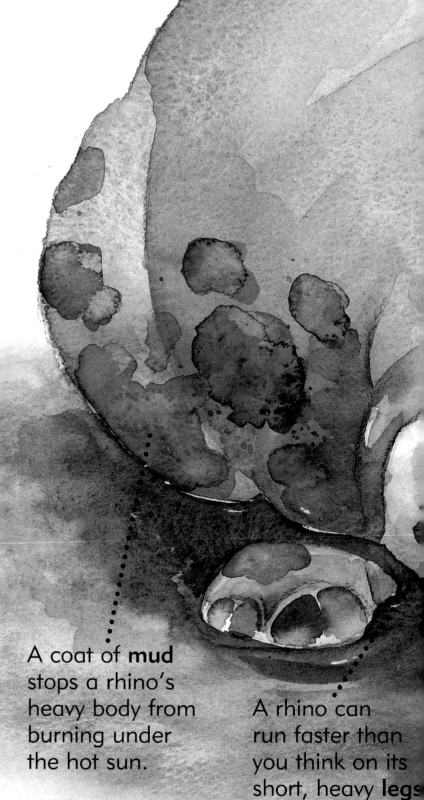

A coat of **mud** stops a rhino's heavy body from burning under the hot sun.

A rhino can run faster than you think on its short, heavy **legs**

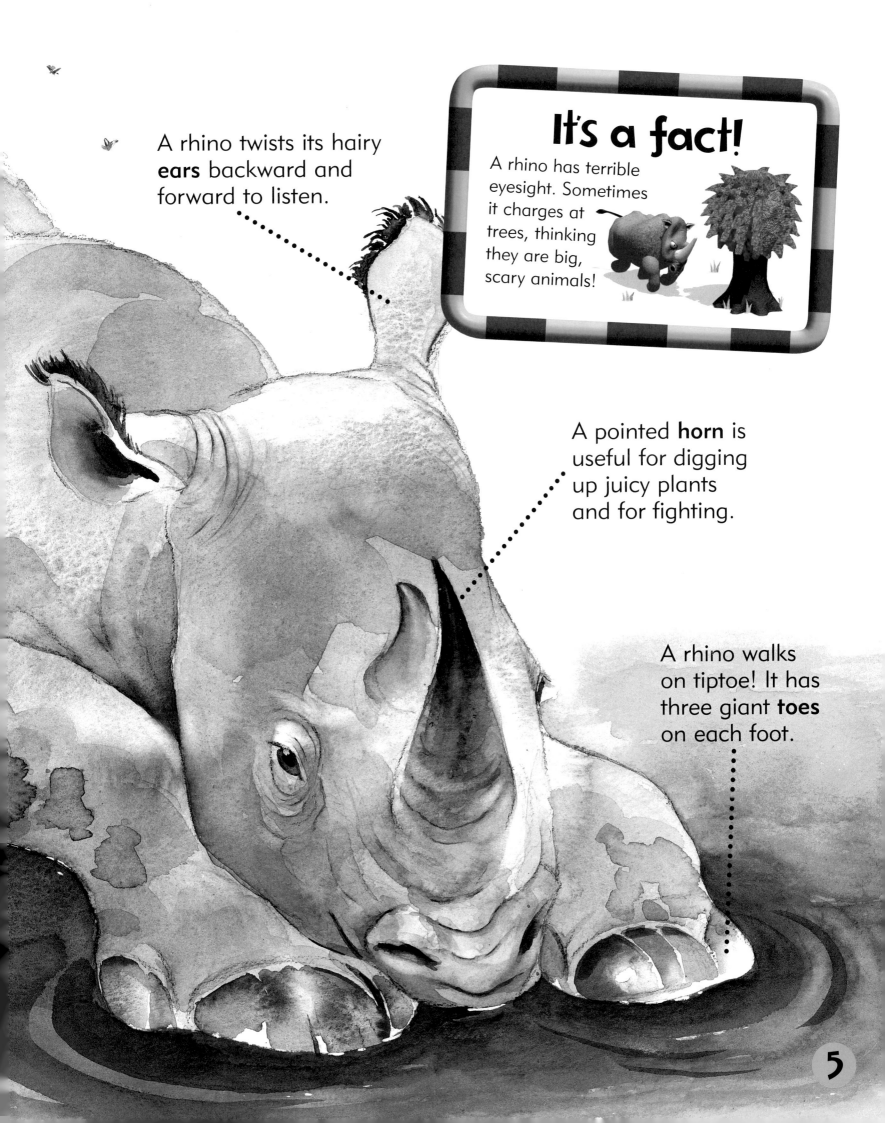

A rhino twists its hairy **ears** backward and forward to listen.

It's a fact!

A rhino has terrible eyesight. Sometimes it charges at trees, thinking they are big, scary animals!

A pointed **horn** is useful for digging up juicy plants and for fighting.

A rhino walks on tiptoe! It has three giant **toes** on each foot.

Giraffe

Small groups of giraffes run across the grasslands on their long, slender legs. They are the tallest animals in the world. Giraffes aren't afraid of many animals, but they have to keep an eye out for hungry lions.

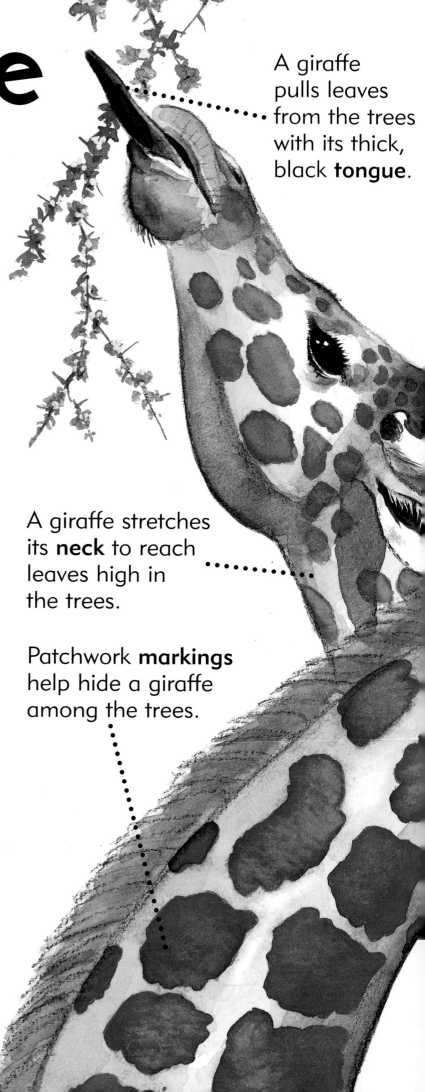

A giraffe pulls leaves from the trees with its thick, black **tongue**.

A giraffe stretches its **neck** to reach leaves high in the trees.

Patchwork **markings** help hide a giraffe among the trees.

A giraffe bends down a long way to drink. It spreads its front legs wide and carefully lowers its head.

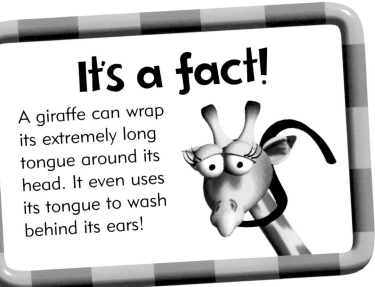

It's a fact!

A giraffe can wrap its extremely long tongue around its head. It even uses its tongue to wash behind its ears!

Two bony **horns** grow from the top of a giraffe's head.

A baby giraffe takes shelter between its mother's legs. Here, it feels snug and safe from enemies.

Thick **eyelashes** protect a giraffe's eyes from wind and dust.

Even the sharpest thorns do not prick a giraffe's thick **lips** as it eats.

Hippopotamus

River hippopotamuses, or hippos for short, love to spend their days lazing around in muddy water. There, they keep cool, away from the hot sun. At night, they climb onto the land to munch grass at the water's edge.

A river hippo has thick, brownish-gray **skin**.

When a river hippo is angry, it opens its big mouth as wide as it can and flashes its long, sharp teeth!

A hippo is an excellent swimmer, but it also enjoys **walking** along the bottom of the river.

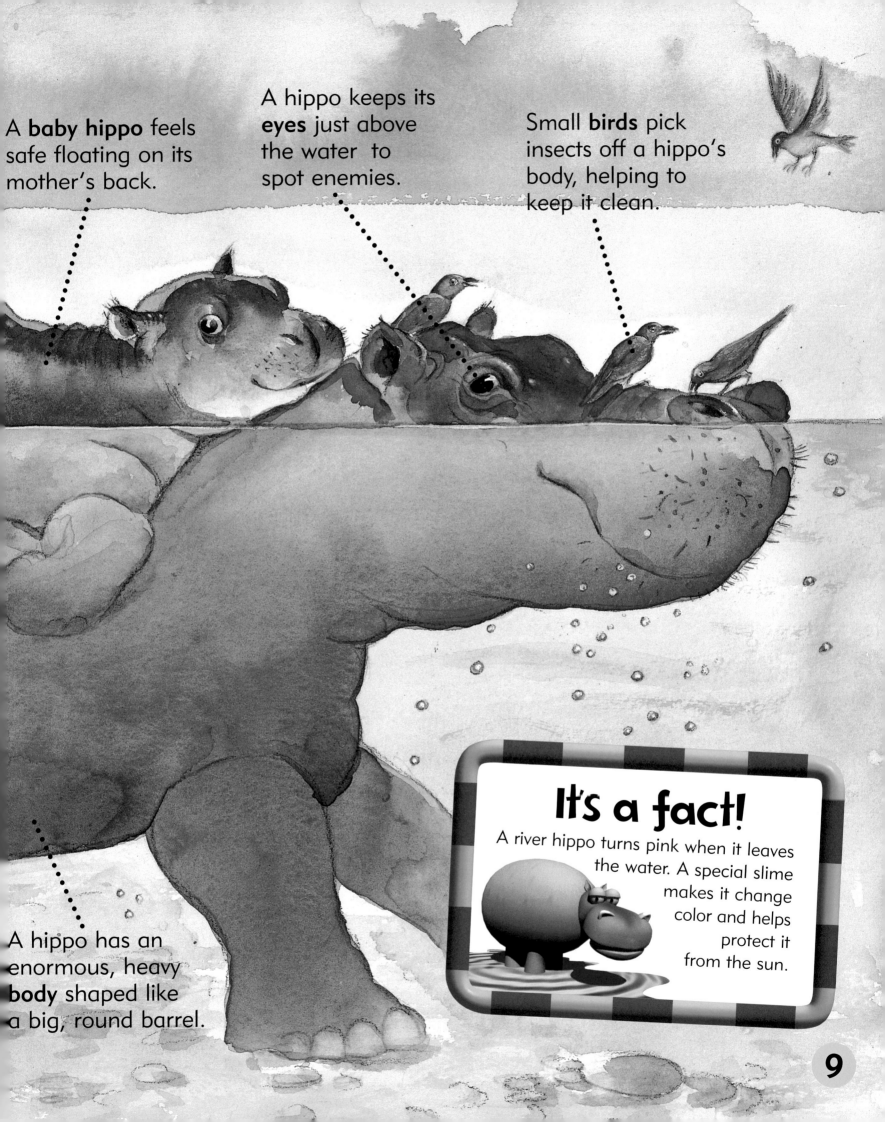

A **baby hippo** feels safe floating on its mother's back.

A hippo keeps its **eyes** just above the water to spot enemies.

Small **birds** pick insects off a hippo's body, helping to keep it clean.

A hippo has an enormous, heavy **body** shaped like a big, round barrel.

It's a fact!

A river hippo turns pink when it leaves the water. A special slime makes it change color and helps protect it from the sun.

 # Zebra

Zebras are quiet animals that gather in groups. They wander around, looking for juicy grass to eat. Zebras are afraid of fierce lions. When they spot a hungry lion, they gallop off as fast as they can!

One zebra **listens** for danger while the others nibble at the grass.

A baby zebra stands up soon after it is born. At first, it wobbles on its long legs, but it quickly learns how to walk.

A zebra brushes away buzzing flies with its long **tail**.

A bony **hoof** covers each foot and protects it like a shoe.

Look closely and you'll see that the black and white **stripes** on each zebra are different!

Groups of zebras often walk for hours across the dry, hot grasslands to drink from a pool of cool water.

Thick tufts of **hair** stick up from a zebra's neck.

Big, flat **teeth** are good for chewing tough clumps of grass.

 # Lion

Lions live together in groups called prides. The females ordinarily do the hunting. They sneak up on their prey and surprise them. After a lion catches a meal, all the members of the pride eat together.

It's a fact!

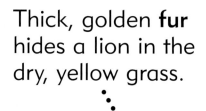

When two lions from the same pride meet, they rub their heads together. This shows that they are friends.

A shaggy **mane** makes a male lion look big and frightening!

Thick, golden **fur** hides a lion in the dry, yellow grass.

A tired lion finds a shady spot in a tree. He sleeps there all day long, away from the hot sun.

Sharp front **teeth**
help a lion catch
and grip its food.

A mighty **roar**
frightens other
animals away.

Baby lions are called cubs. They learn
to be fierce by playing and trying to
fight with their mothers.

A lion quietly creeps
up to its enemies on
its soft, padded **paws**.

By the water

It is busy by the water this morning! Many animals have traveled a long way to take a cool drink.

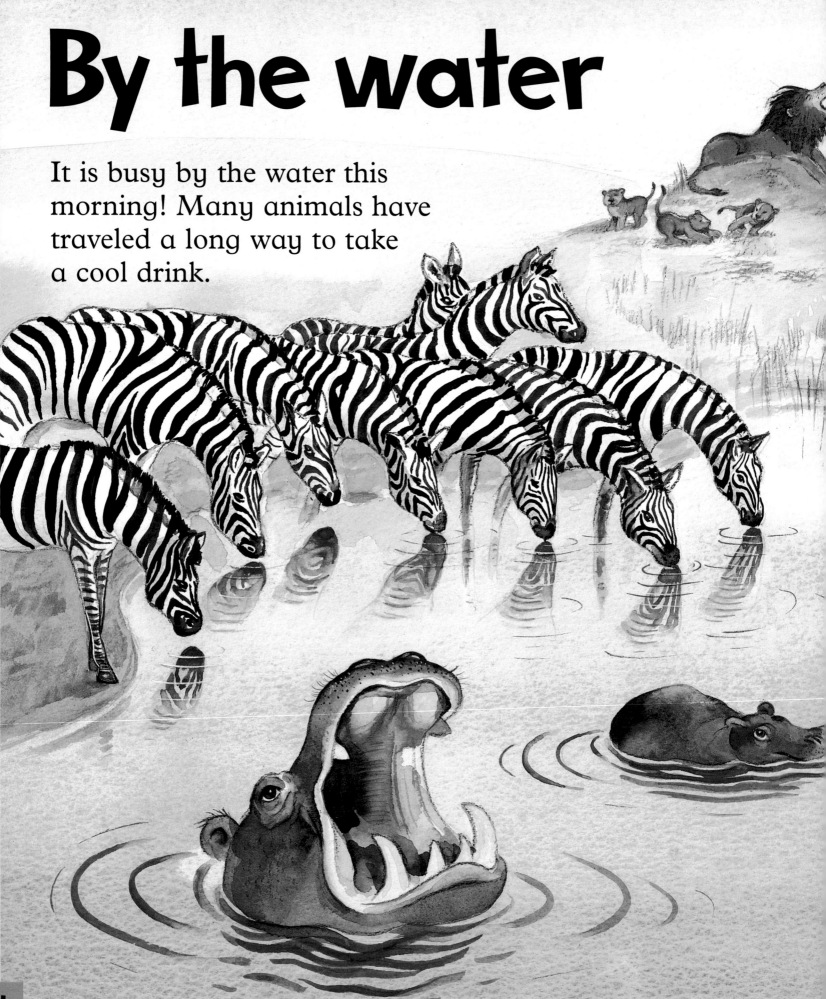

What is the hungry giraffe eating?

Words you know

Here are words that you read earlier in this book. Say them out loud, then find the things in the picture.

hoof	tongue	mane
stripes	skin	horn

15

How does the heavy rhinoceros keep cool?

Elephant

An elephant has the longest nose in the world, but it uses its nose for more than smelling! An elephant uses its nose, called a trunk, for drinking water, carrying food, and making a loud noise just like a trumpet!

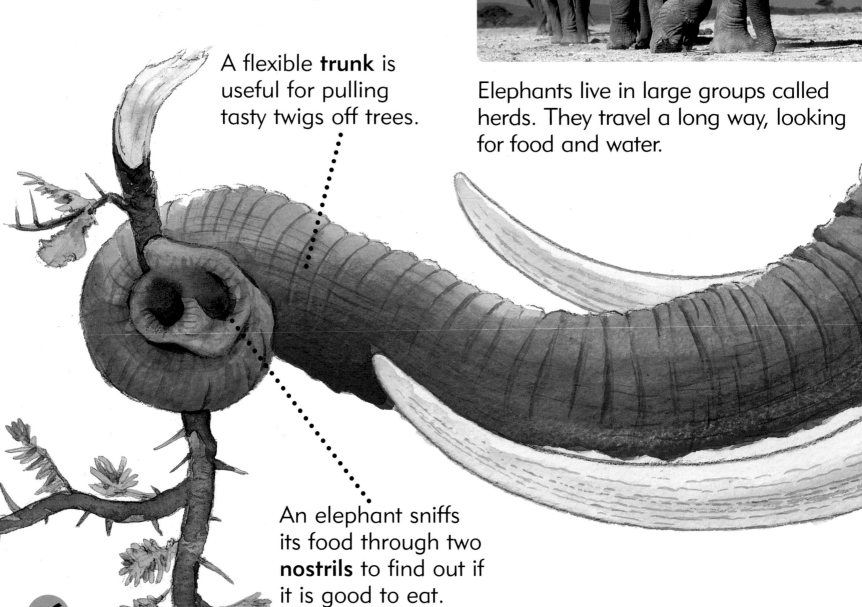

Elephants live in large groups called herds. They travel a long way, looking for food and water.

A flexible **trunk** is useful for pulling tasty twigs off trees.

An elephant sniffs its food through two **nostrils** to find out if it is good to eat.

16

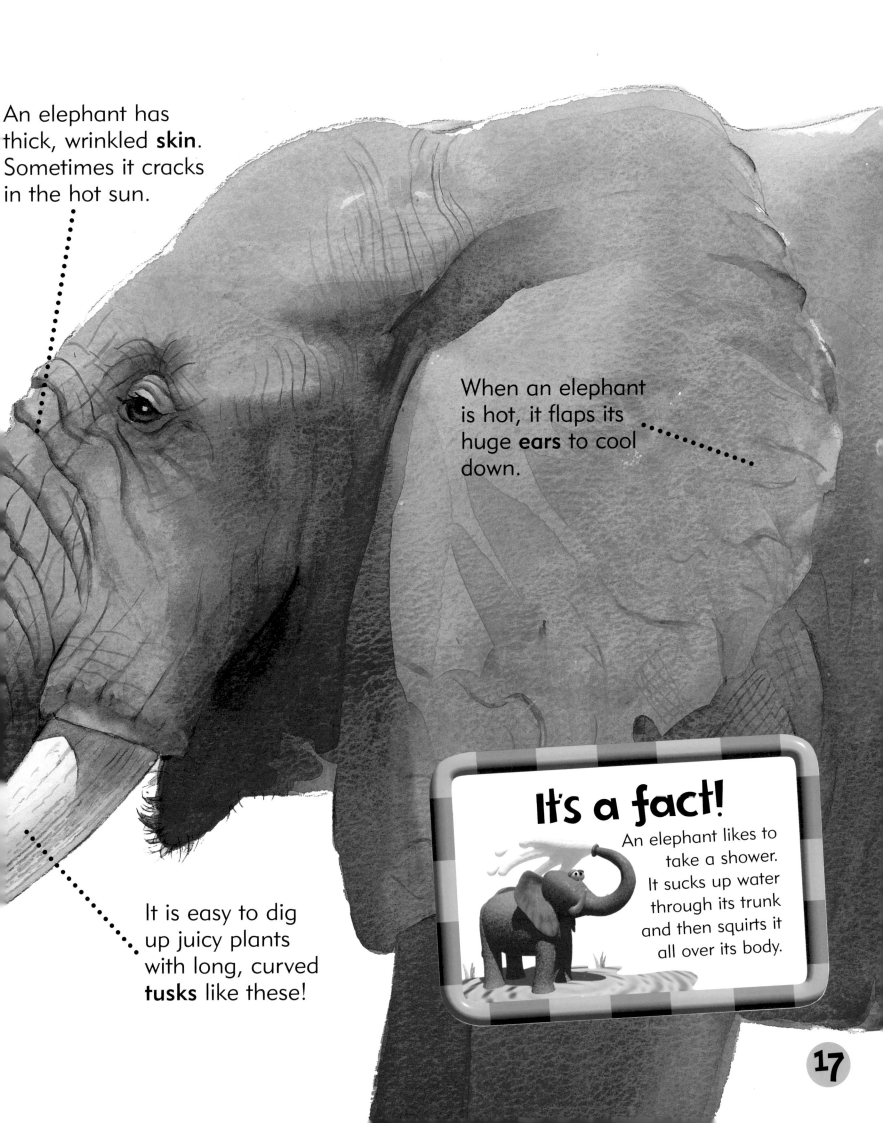

An elephant has thick, wrinkled **skin**. Sometimes it cracks in the hot sun.

When an elephant is hot, it flaps its huge **ears** to cool down.

It is easy to dig up juicy plants with long, curved **tusks** like these!

It's a fact!

An elephant likes to take a shower. It sucks up water through its trunk and then squirts it all over its body.

Cheetah

During the day, a sneaky cheetah hunts for its dinner. It spots an animal from far away and follows it silently through the grass. Then the cheetah leaps out and chases it as fast as it can. In seconds, the cheetah has a tasty meal!

When a cheetah turns, it holds out its **tail**. This keeps the cheetah steady.

A yellow coat with black **spots** hides a cheetah as it moves through the grass.

It's a fact!

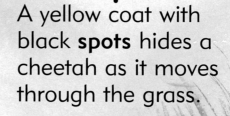

A cheetah runs faster than any other animal on land. Over short distances, it runs as fast as a car on a highway!

Powerful, long **legs**, such as these, are best for running quickly.

Many animals are afraid of this sharp **bite**!

Strong **claws** dig into the hard ground. Like athletic shoes with cleats, they help a cheetah run fast.

A mother cheetah looks after her silver-haired baby for many months, teaching it how to live in the wild.

 # Chimpanzee

Chimpanzees, or chimps for short, live in noisy groups. They look after one another and search for food together. When they are excited, they jump up and down and scream as loudly as they can.

A piggyback ride keeps a **baby chimp** safe from harm.

Young chimpanzees enjoy playing in the trees. They grip the branches tightly with their hands and feet.

A **stick** is useful for digging up ants to eat.

Keeping clean is easy. The mother picks twigs out of the baby chimp's fur.

Chimpanzees **make faces** to communicate with each other.

A chimpanzee walks on all fours, leaning on its **knuckles**.

It's a fact!

A chimpanzee makes its own bed! Each night, it climbs up a tree and lays down twigs and leaves where it sleeps.

 # Amazing birds

There are hundreds of amazing birds on the grasslands. Giant ostriches run along the ground and tiny, colorful weavers fly from tree to tree. You may even spot a hungry vulture swooping through the sky.

A vulture spots a snack from far away with a pair of beady **eyes**.

Silky **feathers** cover a vulture's body and keep it warm and dry.

A hooked **beak** is for tearing up chunks of food.

Ostriches cannot fly, but they can run very fast on their long, skinny legs.

It's a fact!

An ostrich lays the strongest eggs in the world. If you jump up and down on one, it still won't crack!

To fly, a vulture stretches out its two huge **wings**.

A vulture can pick up tasty meals with its strong, clawed **feet**.

A weaver works hard to build its nest. It collects strips of grass and weaves them into a ball on a branch.

Roaming around

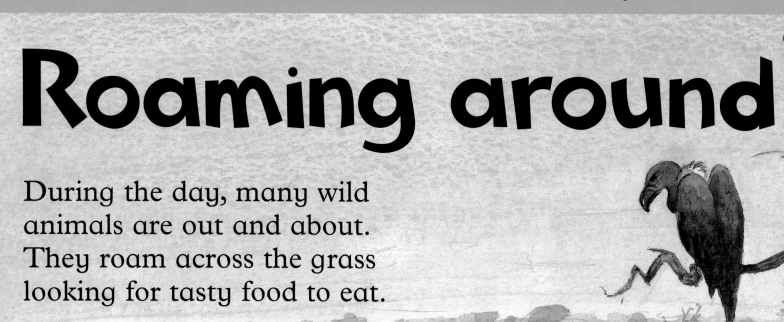

During the day, many wild animals are out and about. They roam across the grass looking for tasty food to eat.

How many spotted cheetahs are hiding in the grass?

24

Which noisy animals are swinging through the trees?

Words you know

Here are words that you read earlier in this book. Say them out loud, then find the things in the picture.

tusks   trunk   tail
feathers   beak   wings

25

Did you know?

Fewer than 15,000 cheetahs remain in the wild.

A zebra's large ears rotate to locate sounds, and its night vision is as good as an owl's.

Mother chimpanzees often develop lifelong relationships with their babies, as human mothers do.

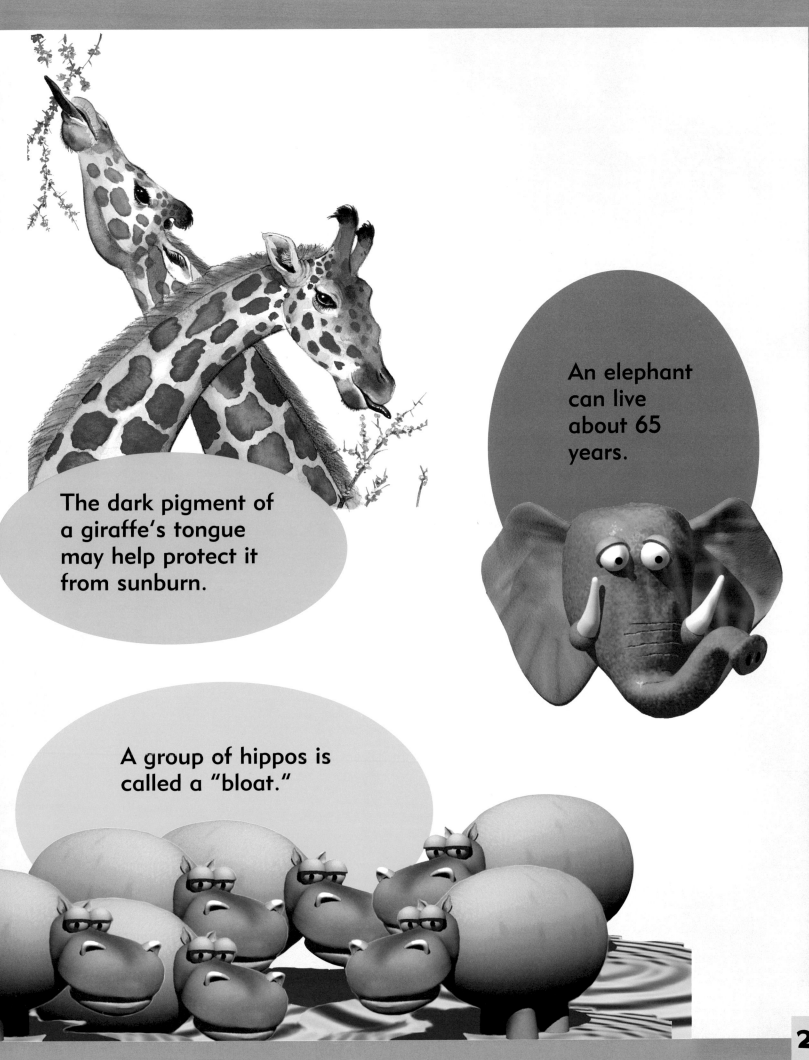

The dark pigment of a giraffe's tongue may help protect it from sunburn.

An elephant can live about 65 years.

A group of hippos is called a "bloat."

Puzzles

Close-up!

We've zoomed in on parts of some animals' bodies. Can you figure out which animals you are looking at?

1

2

3

Answers on page 32.

Whose coat?

These animals have lost their patterned coats! Can you match each animal to its coat?

1

2

3

giraffe

cheetah

zebra

28

Match up!

Match each word on the left with its picture on the right.

a

1. rhinoceros

b

2. ostrich

c

3. vulture

d

4. elephant

e

5. lion cub

6. chimpanzee

f

Answers on page 32.

True or false

Can you figure out which animals are telling the truth? You can go to the page numbers listed to find out the answers.

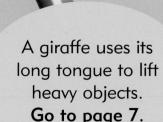

A cheetah can run as fast as a car. **Go to page 18.**

1

A giraffe uses its long tongue to lift heavy objects. **Go to page 7.**

3

2

When two lions from the same pride meet, they rub heads to show they are friends. **Go to page 12.**

4

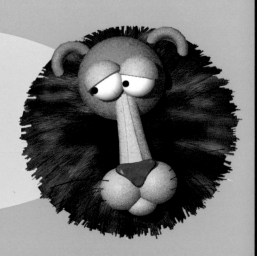

River hippos turn green when they leave the water. **Go to page 9.**

A chimpanzee makes its own bed each night in a tree. **Go to page 21.**

5

Answers on page 32.

Find out more

Books

All About Wild Animals (Gareth Stevens, 2004-2005) 22 volumes
Each volume tells about a different animal: what it looks like, how it cares for its young, and what it eats. Titles include *Camels*, *Kangaroos*, and *Zebras*.

Animal Scavengers, Sandra Markle (Lerner, 2005) 6 volumes
Find out how army ants, hyenas, jackals, Tasmanian devils, vultures, and wolverines get their food.

Ostriches, Caroline Arnold (Lerner, 2001)
Read about the fascinating body and life of the ostrich.

Wild World (Heinemann Library, 2006) 13 volumes
In addition to basic information about 13 different animals, a "Tracker's Guide" identifies signs of the animal's presence, such as foot tracks and droppings.

World of Mammals (Child's World, 2006) 12 volumes
Learn about the dangers that threaten the lives of 12 wild animals, each presented in one of the books in this set.

Websites

Animal Database, by Kids Biology
http://www.kidsbiology.com/animals-for-children.php
Learn about hundreds of different animals, from anteaters, armadillos, and aardvarks to songbirds, turtles, and whales. Each animal page includes a photograph and a list of animal facts.

Creature Feature Archive, National Geographic Kids Magazine
http://www.nationalgeographic.com/kids/creature_feature/archive
Learn about such wild animals as bats, lemurs, and warthogs. Each feature includes fun facts, pictures, sound bites, and a map that shows where the creature lives.

Jungle Photos
http://junglephotos.com
Choose from three jungle regions of the world—Africa, the Amazon, and the Galapagos Islands—and click on "Animals" to get great photos of unusual animals.

Southeastern Raptors for Kids, Southeastern Raptor Center
http://www.vetmed.auburn.edu/home/programs-and-centers/southeastern-raptor-center/for-kids
Get to know the raptors—meat-eating birds.

Answers

Puzzles
from pages 28 and 29

Close-up!
1. vulture
2. elephant
3. lion

Whose coat?
1. cheetah
2. giraffe
3. zebra

Match up!
1. c
2. a
3. d
4. f
5. e
6. b

True or false
from page 30

1. true
2. false
3. false
4. true
5. true

Index